WHO MADE MY LUNCH?
FROM GROVE TO FRUIT SALAD

BY MARI SCHUH · ILLUSTRATED BY JEANINE MURCH

AMICUS ILLUSTRATED is published by Amicus Learning, an imprint of Amicus P.O. Box 227, Mankato, MN 56002 www.amicuspublishing.us

© 2025 Amicus. International copyright reserved in all countries. No part of this book may be reproduced in any form without written permission from the publisher.

LIBRARY OF CONGRESS CATALOGING-IN-PUBLICATION DATA
Names: Schuh, Mari C., 1975- author. | Murch, Jeanine Henderson, illustrator.
Title: From grove to fruit salad / by Mari Schuh ; illustrated by Jeanine Murch.
Description: Mankato, MN : Amicus Illustrated, [2025] | Series: Who made my lunch? | Includes bibliographical references. | Audience: Ages 6-9 | Audience: Grades 2-3 | Summary: "A child wonders where fruit comes from and learns about farming oranges, apples, strawberries, and bananas and how they are packaged and transported to grocery stores. This illustrated narrative nonfiction book includes a world map of where these fruits are grown, glossary, and further resources, making it a great story to support farm-to-table education"— Provided by publisher.
Identifiers: LCCN 2024010617 (print) | LCCN 2024010618 (ebook) | ISBN 9798892001106 (library binding) | ISBN 9798892001687 (paperback) | ISBN 9798892002264 (ebook)
Subjects: LCSH: Fruit—Juvenile literature. | Fruit salads—Juvenile literature. | Orchards—Juvenile literature.
Classification: LCC TX558.F7 S378 2025 (print) | LCC TX558.F7 (ebook) | DDC 641.3/4—dc23/eng/20240327
LC record available at https://lccn.loc.gov/2024010617
LC ebook record available at https://lccn.loc.gov/2024010618

EDITOR: Rebecca Glaser
SERIES DESIGNER: Kathleen Petelinsek
BOOK DESIGNER: Kim Pfeffer

Printed in China

FOR ELLA AND MAX—M.S.

ABOUT THE AUTHOR
Mari Schuh's love of reading began with cereal boxes at the kitchen table. Today she is the author of hundreds of nonfiction books for beginning readers. She lives in the Midwest with her husband and their sassy house rabbit. Apples are Mari's favorite fruit, while tiny banana pieces are her rabbit's favorite.

ABOUT THE ILLUSTRATOR
Jeanine Murch is an illustrator with a lifelong love of art, books, and storytelling. She lives in Pittsburgh, PA, with her husband, two children, and the world's most snuggly pup, all of which inspire her work. When she isn't making art, she's usually daydreaming about her next travel adventure.

So tasty and sweet! A fruit salad is a healthy part of lunch. But what if you had to grow the oranges, apples, strawberries, and bananas yourself?

Find your hat and go to warm, sunny California. It grows the most oranges in the U.S. As a farmer, you'll need a large grove of orange trees and a lot of time. An orange tree grows for about five years before it grows fruit.

After that, most oranges take about six to eight months to ripen. Finally! These navel oranges are ripe. Pick them by hand. Gently clip them off at the stem. Then put them into bags and bins.

Next up, the packing house. Here, machines wash, dry, and sort the oranges. Cameras take pictures of each orange. A worker reviews the pictures. These oranges are healthy!

Packing time! Machines and workers pack the oranges into bags and boxes. Then they are shipped to grocery stores for people to buy and enjoy.

Next up, strawberries. Good news! You don't need to go far. Stay in California and travel to the coast. There, you'll find huge fields of strawberries growing all year. Put on a big hat and start picking!

While you're in the field, put the strawberries into small containers. Do not wash the strawberries. Water could make them rotten and soft.

Cool the strawberries to keep them fresh. Take them to a cooling facility, where strong fans blow cold air around the strawberries. Then deliver them to grocery stores in refrigerated trucks. It takes just a few days to go from the field to the store!

Want some crisp red apples? Go north! Travel to Washington, which grows the most apples in the U.S. The soil and climate make it a perfect place for apple orchards.

You need to plan way ahead. Apple trees start growing fruit in their third year. In early spring, blossoms grow. Bees pollinate the blossoms. Then all summer, your apples grow.

August is here. Time to harvest! Apples can easily bruise. Workers carefully pick them by hand.

Deliver the apples to a processing facility. There, the apples are inspected, washed, and dried. They are sorted by size and type. After they are packaged, trucks deliver the apples to stores around the country.

Of course, you'll want some bananas. After all, they are the world's most popular fruit. Bananas grow best in tropical areas. Buy a plane ticket to Guatemala. It's the biggest grower of bananas for the U.S.

Banana plants grow all year on big farms. Bananas need time to grow. In nine months, they will be ready to harvest. Use a big knife to cut down bunches of green, unripe bananas.

Take the bananas to a packing shed. There, the bananas are inspected and washed. All aboard! Ships take the bananas on a long trip. The bananas are kept cool so they don't ripen early.

The ship arrives at a port, where the bananas are loaded onto trucks. Next, they are taken to a facility and put in a sealed room. Ethylene gas is pumped in to help the bananas ripen. In a few days, they're ready for the grocery store!

Thanks to the fruit growers, fruit pickers, factory workers, and truck drivers, you have a colorful bowl of fruit salad to enjoy. Grab a fork and dig in!

WHERE ARE COMMON FRUITS GROWN?

GLOSSARY

climate The weather of a place over a long period of time.

ethylene A gas that is used to ripen fruits.

facility A building for a certain activity, such as inspecting or sorting fruit.

inspect To look at something closely and carefully.

pollinate To move pollen from flower to flower, which helps plants grow.

port A place where ships go to load and unload supplies.

ripen Becoming fully grown and ready to eat.

tropical Having a hot and wet climate. Tropical areas are near the equator.

WEBSITES

Kids Fruit: B Is for Bananas
https://www.kidsfruit.org/get-learning/b-is-for/
Learn where bananas are grown and how they get from the field to your kitchen.

NIEHS Kids' Pages: Apples and Oranges
https://kids.niehs.nih.gov/games/songs/childrens/apples-and-oranges
Enjoy a fun song about apples and oranges.

Washington Apple Commission: Apple Games & Puzzles for Kids
https://waapple.org/apple-games-puzzles-for-kids/
Word search games, crossword puzzles, and coloring sheets.

Every effort has been made to ensure that these websites are appropriate for children. However, because of the nature of the Internet, it is impossible to guarantee that these sites will remain active indefinitely or that their contents will not be altered.

READ MORE

Culliford, Amy. *Oranges.* New York: Crabtree Publishing, 2024.

Marsico, Katie. *Fantastic Fruit.* Ann Arbor, Mich.: Cherry Lake Publishing, 2021.

Quick, J.F. *Apples.* Mankato, Minn.: Creative Education and Creative Paperbacks, 2025.